# STRUM & SING

# CHART HITS
# OF 2015-2016

ISBN 978-1-4950-5823-3

**HAL•LEONARD®**
CORPORATION

7777 W. BLUEMOUND RD. P.O. BOX 13819 MILWAUKEE, WI 53213

Visit Hal Leonard Online at
**www.halleonard.com**

# Adventure of a Lifetime

Words and Music by
Guy Berryman, Jon Buckland,
Chris Martin, Will Champion,
Mikkel Eriksen and Tor Hermansen

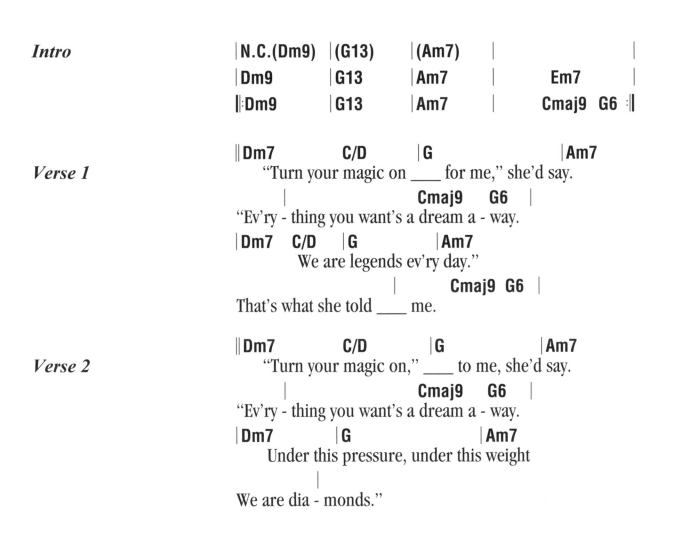

**Intro**

|N.C.(Dm9) |(G13) |(Am7) | | |
|Dm9 |G13 |Am7 | Em7 |
‖:Dm9 |G13 |Am7 | Cmaj9  G6 :‖

**Verse 1**

‖Dm7          C/D      |G                    |Am7
  "Turn your magic on ____ for me," she'd say.
     |                              Cmaj9   G6   |
  "Ev'ry - thing you want's a dream a - way.
|Dm7    C/D   |G            |Am7
      We are legends ev'ry day."
              |              Cmaj9   G6   |
That's what she told ____ me.

**Verse 2**

‖Dm7          C/D      |G            |Am7
  "Turn your magic on," ____ to me, she'd say.
     |                          Cmaj9   G6   |
  "Ev'ry - thing you want's a dream a - way.
|Dm7          |G                |Am7
  Under this pressure, under this weight
              |
We are dia - monds."

*Chorus 1*

```
        Cmaj9   G6      ‖Dm7            C/D  |
And I feel      my heart ___ beating.
|G                   |Am7                    |
I feel my heart ___ beneath my skin.
|       Cmaj9  G6     |N.C.(Dm7) |
I feel       my heart ___ beating.
| (G)                     |Am7        |
Oh, you make me feel
|               Em7   |Dm7    C/D |G          |
Like I'm a - live again.
|Am7        |       Cmaj9  G6        |Dm7    C/D |
           (A - live a   -    gain.)
|G                   |Am7            |
Oh, you make me feel
|             Cmaj9  G6       |
Like I'm a - live a   -   gain.
```

*Verse 3*

```
‖Dm7      C/D          |G          |Am7       |
    Said, I can't go on, ___ not in this way.
       |             Cmaj9  G6  |
I'm a dream, I die by light of  day.
|Dm7      C/D   |G            |Am7       |
Gonna hold up half the sky and say,
                  |
"Only I own ___ me."
```

*Chorus 2*

```
        Cmaj9   G6      ‖Dm7            C/D  |
And I feel      my heart ___ beating.
|G                   |Am7                    |
I feel my heart ___ beneath my skin.
|               Cmaj9  G6       |N.C.(Dm7) |
Oh, I can feel      my heart ___ beating,
| (G)                     |Am7        |
'Cause you make me feel
|             Em7   |Dm7    C/D |G          |
Like I'm a - live again.
|Am7        |       Cmaj9  G6        |Dm7    C/D |
           (A - live a   -    gain.)
|G                   |Am7            |
Oh, you make me feel
|             Cmaj9  G6       |
Like I'm a - live a   -   gain.
```

*Interlude 1*     ‖ Dm7     | G13     | Am7     |     G     |

*Verse 4*     ‖ Dm7                         | G                     | Am7

         "Turn your magic on ___ for me," she'd say.
          |                     G                 |
       "Ev'ry - thing you want's a dream away.
        | Dm7             | G                     | Am7
          Under this pressure, under this weight
           |             G             | A5
      We are dia - monds taking shape,
           |             Em7             |
      We are dia - monds taking shape."

*Interlude 2*     | Dm7  C/D  | G             | Am7     |     Cmaj9     G6   |
              | Dm7  C/D  | G             | Am7     |

*Bridge*     |             Cmaj9     G6  ‖ Dm7             C/D         |
             If we've ___ on - ly got this ___ life
 | G                     | Am7                     |
      And this adven - ture, oh, then I…
     |         Cmaj9     G6  | Dm7             C/D         |
     And if we've ___ on - ly got this ___ life,
 | G                             | Am7     |
      You'll get me through, ___ oh.
     |         Cmaj9     G6  | Dm7             C/D         |
     And if we've ___ on - ly got this ___ life
 | G                     | Am7     |
      And this adven - ture, oh, then
     |             Cmaj9     G6  | Dm7     C/D     | G
 I ___ wanna share it  with  you,     with   you,
        | Am7                 |         Cmaj9  G6   |
 With you. Sing it, oh, ___ sing, yeah.     Woo-

*Outro*     ‖: Dm7                     C/D  | G
       Hoo. (Woo-hoo.) Woo - hoo. (Woo-hoo.)
        | Am7                     |                 Cmaj9  G6     :‖
 Woo-hoo. (Woo-hoo.) Woo-hoo. (Woo-hoo.)     Woo-
 | Dm9                         | G
       Hoo. (Woo-hoo.) Woo-hoo. (Woo-hoo.)
        | Am7                     | N.C.                     ‖
 Woo-hoo. (Woo-hoo.) Woo-hoo. (Woo-hoo.)

# Can't Feel My Face

Words and Music by
Abel Tesfaye, Max Martin,
Savan Kotecha, Peter Svensson
and Ali Payami

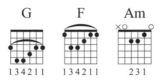

**Intro**  |G    |F    |Am         |

**Verse 1**
               |G
And I know ___ she'll be the death of me,
       |F
At least ___ we'll both be numb.
            |Am                        |
And she'll al - ways get the best of me, the worst is yet to come.
          |G                                      |F
But at least ___ we'll both be beautiful and stay ___ forever young.
         |Am              |
This I know, ___ yeah, this I know.

**Pre-Chorus 1**

|G                      |F
She told me, "Don't worry about ___ it."
             |Am          |
She told me, "Don't worry no more."
              |G               |F
We both know we can't go without ___ it.
             |Am              |
She told me, "You'll never be alone."
|           |
Oh, oh, ooh.

**Chorus 1**

|G                                      |F
I can't feel my face when I'm with you,
         |Am          |
But I love ___ it, but I love it.
  |G                                    |F
Oh, I can't feel my face when I'm with you,
         |Am          |                          ||
But I love ___ it, but I love it.

**Verse 2**

                    |N.C.
And I know ___ she'll be the death of me,
         |F
At least ___ we'll both be numb.
              |Am                            |
And she'll al - ways get the best of me, the worst is yet to come.
              |G                    |F
All the mis - ery was necessary when ___ we're deep in love.
             |Am          |
This I know, ___ girl, I know.

**Pre-Chorus 2**     *Repeat Pre-Chorus 1*

*Chorus 2*

‖:**G**                                                    |**F**
I can't feel my face when I'm with you,
          |**Am**                    |
But I love ____ it, but I love it.
   |**G**                                                |**F**
Oh, I can't feel my face when I'm with you,
          |**Am**                    |            :‖
But I love ____ it, but I love it.  Oh.


*Interlude*        |**G**                    |**F**                    |**Am**                    |                    |


*Pre-Chorus 3*
          |**Am**                          |**G**                |**F**
          She told me, "Don't worry about ____ it."
                              |**Am**            |
She told me, "Don't worry no more."
                              |**G**                |**F**
We both know we can't go without ____ it.
                              |**Am**                    |
She told me, "You'll never be alone."
|        |**N.C.**        |
Oh, oh.        *Ooh!*


*Chorus 3*

‖:**G**                                                    |**F**
I can't feel my face when I'm with you,
          |**Am**                    |
But I love ____ it, but I love it.
   |**G**                                                |**F**
Oh, I can't feel my face when I'm with you,
          |**Am**                    |            :‖
But I love ____ it, but I love it.  Oh.


*Outro*        |**G**                    |**F**                    |**Am**                    |                    ‖

                                                                        Hey!

9

# Budapest

Words and Music by
George Barnett and Joel Pott

Tune down 1 step:
(low to high) D-G-C-F-A-D

G     C     D

*Intro*

|| G | | | |

*Verse 1*

|| G | |
    My house in Budapest, my, ___ my hidden treasure chest,
| | |
    Golden grand piano, ___ my beautiful Castillo.
| C | | G | |
You, hoo, you, oo, I'd leave it all.
| | |
    My acres of a, land    I've achieved,
| |
    It may be hard for you to ___ stop and believe.
| C | | G |
But for you, hoo, you, oo, I'd leave it all.
| | C | | G | |
    Oh, for you, hoo, you, oo, I'd leave it all.

*Chorus 1*

|| D
  Gimme one good reason
| C | G | |
Why I ___ should never make a change.
| D | C | G | |
    Baby, if you hold me then all ___ of this will go away.

*Verse 2*

|| G | |
    My many artifacts, ___ the list goes on.
| | |
    If you just say the words, I, ___ I'll up and run on to
| C | | G |
You, hoo, you, oo, I'd leave it all.
| | C | | G | |
    Oh, for you, hoo, you, oo, I'd leave it all.

**Chorus 2**

‖ **D**

  Gimme one good reason

      | **C**                              | **G**        |        |

Why I ___ should never make a change.

| **D**                    | **C**            | **G**        |      |

 Baby, if you hold me then all ___ of this will go away.

| **D**

 Gimme one good reason

      | **C**                              | **G**        |        |

Why I ___ should never make a change.

| **D**                    | **C**            | **G**        |      |

 Baby, if you hold me then all ___ of this will go away.

**Interlude**

‖ **G**        |        |        |        |

| **C**        |        | **G**        |        |

**Verse 3**

‖ **G**                              |           |

     My friends and family, they ___ don't understand.

|                            |

     They fear they'll lose so much if ___ you take my hand.

     | **C**        |     | **G**        |

But for you, hoo, you, oo, I'd lose it all.

|       | **C**        |     | **G**        |     |

   Oh, for you, hoo, you, oo, I'd lose it all.

**Chorus 3**

*Repeat Chorus 2*

**Outro-Verse**

‖ **G**                              |            |

     My house in Budapest, my, ___ my hidden treasure chest,

|               |            |

     Golden grand piano, ___ my beautiful Castillo.

| **C**        |     | **G**        |

 You, hoo, you, oo, I'd leave it all.

|       | **C**        |     | **G**        ‖

   Oh, for you, hoo, you, oo, I'd leave it all.

# Burning House

Words and Music by
Jeff Bhasker, Tyler Sam Johnson
and Camaron Ochs

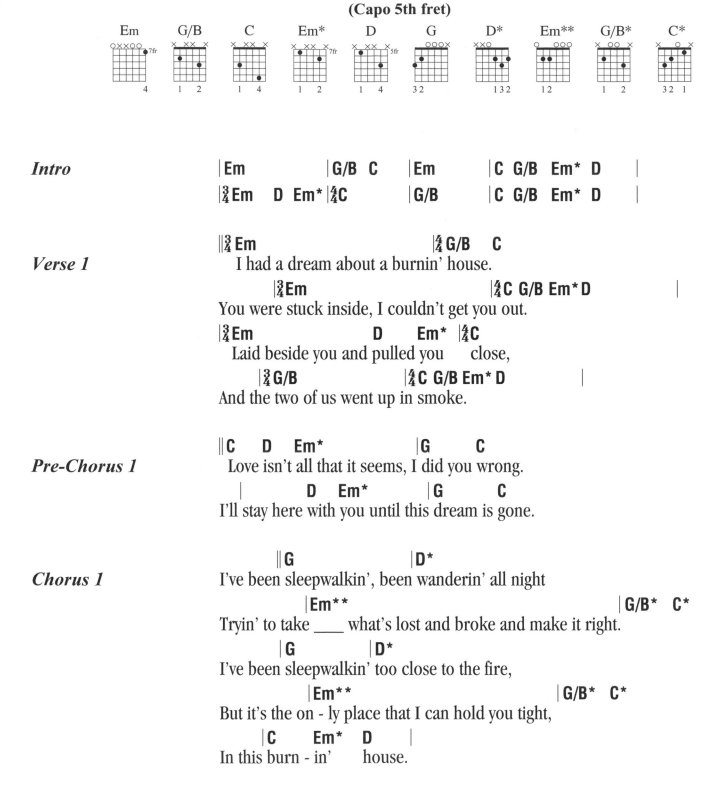

**(Capo 5th fret)**

Em    G/B    C    Em*    D    G    D*    Em**    G/B*    C*

*Intro*

|Em          |G/B C    |Em          |C G/B Em* D          |

|3/4 Em    D    Em* |4/4 C          |G/B          |C G/B Em* D          |

*Verse 1*

|3/4 Em                          |4/4 G/B    C
     I had a dream about a burnin' house.

       |3/4 Em                          |4/4 C G/B Em* D          |
You were stuck inside, I couldn't get you out.

|3/4 Em                    D    Em* |4/4 C
    Laid beside you and pulled you     close,

       |3/4 G/B                    |4/4 C G/B Em* D          |
And the two of us went up in smoke.

*Pre-Chorus 1*

||C    D    Em*          |G          C
    Love isn't all that it seems, I did you wrong.

   |          D    Em*    |G          C
I'll stay here with you until this dream is gone.

*Chorus 1*

       ||G                    |D*
I've been sleepwalkin', been wanderin' all night

       |Em**                          |G/B*    C*
Tryin' to take ___ what's lost and broke and make it right.

       |G          |D*
I've been sleepwalkin' too close to the fire,

       |Em**                          |G/B*    C*
But it's the on - ly place that I can hold you tight,

       |C    Em*    D    |
In this burn - in'    house.

*Verse 2*

```
   ||¾Em                         D   Em*|⁴⁄₄C
     See you at a party and you look the    same.
       |¾Em                            |⁴⁄₄C G/B Em* D            |
   I could take you back but people don't ev - er  change.
   |¾Em                   D   Em* |⁴⁄₄C
    Wish that we could go back in       time.
     |¾G/B                   |⁴⁄₄C G/B Em* D            |
   I'd be the one you thought you'd find.
```

*Pre-Chorus 2*     *Repeat Pre-Chorus 1*

*Chorus 2*     *Repeat Chorus 1*

*Bridge*

```
   ||G/B*                C          |      Em*  D
    Flames are gettin' big - ger now in this burn - in'    house.
            |G/B*             C          |     Em*   D
   I can hold ___ on to you some - how in this burn - in'    house.
         |G                 C*         |     Em*  D      |
   Oh, and I don't wanna wake ___ up in this burn - in'    house.
```

*Chorus 3*

```
   |²⁄₄N.C.        ||⁴⁄₄G            |D*
     And I've been sleepwalkin', been wanderin' all night
            |Em**                          |G/B*  C*
   Tryin' to take ___ what's lost and broke and make it right.
         |G         |D*
   I've been sleepwalkin' too close to the fire,
          |Em**                         |G/B*  C*
   But it's the on - ly place that I can hold you tight,
      |C      Em*   D*     ||
   In this burn - in'   house.
```

# Die a Happy Man

Words and Music by
Thomas Rhett, Joe Spargur
and Sean Douglas

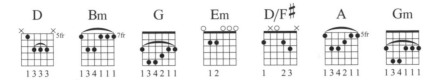

**Intro**
> |D　Bm　|G　D　|　Bm　|G　D

**Verse 1**
> ‖D　　　Bm　|G　D
> Baby, last night　　was, hands down,
> |　　　　Bm　　|G　D
> One of the best nights　　that I've had, no doubt,
> |　　　　Bm
> Between the bottle of wine and the look in your eyes
> |G　D
> And the Marvin Gaye.
> |　　　　Bm
> Then we danced in the dark under September stars
> |G　D
> In the pourin' rain.

**Pre-Chorus 1**
> ‖Em　D/F♯　　|G　D
> And I know that I can't ever tell you e - nough
> |Em　D/F♯　　|G　A
> That all I need in this life is your crazy love.

**Chorus 1**

```
      ‖Bm              |G        D
If I never get to see the Northern Lights,
         |Bm                    |G       D
Or if I never get to see the Eiffel Tower at night,
         |Bm          |G        D           |
Oh, if all I got is your hand in my hand, baby,
|Bm        |G   D   |    Bm     |
 I could die a happy man,
|G         D           |   Bm  |G      D
     A happy man, baby.
```

**Verse 2**

```
         ‖D      Bm        |G    D
Baby, that red dress    brings me to my knees.
          |         Bm         |G       D
Oh, but that black dress    makes it hard to breathe.
          |              Bm
You're a saint, you're a god - dess,
                    |G        D
The cutest, the hottest, a master - piece.
          |             Bm
It's too good to be true, nothin' better than you
          |G      D
In my wildest dreams.
```

**Pre-Chorus 2**      *Repeat Pre-Chorus 1*

**Chorus 2**

```
      ‖Bm              |G        D
If I never get to see the Northern Lights,
         |Bm                    |G        D
Or if I never get to see the Eiffel Tower at night,
         |Bm          |G        D          |
Oh, if all I got is your hand in my hand, baby,
|Bm        |G   D              |
 I could die a happy man, yeah, yeah.
```

**Slide Guitar Solo**      *Repeat Intro*

*Bridge*

```
     ‖G                    |Gm
I don't need no vacation, no fancy destination.
     |D                    |Bm
Baby, you're my great escape.
       |G                    |Gm        |
We could stay at home, listen to the radio,
|D                    |A
 Dance around the fireplace.
```

*Chorus 3*

```
       ‖Bm                |G         D
Oh, if I never get to build my mansion in Georgia
         |Bm                    |G     D
Or drive a sports car up the coast of Cali - fornia,
       |Bm          |G        D
Oh, if all I got is your hand in my hand,
         |Bm          |G     D
Baby, I ____ could die a happy man.
         |Bm          |G     D
Baby, I ____ could die a happy man.
       |Bm          |G    D
Oh, I could die a happy man.
                        |     Bm     |
You know I could, girl.
|G          D                    |    Bm  |G    D  ‖
    I could die, I could die a happy man.
```

16

# Ex's & Oh's

Words and Music by
Tanner Schneider and Dave Bassett

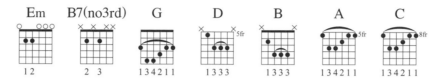

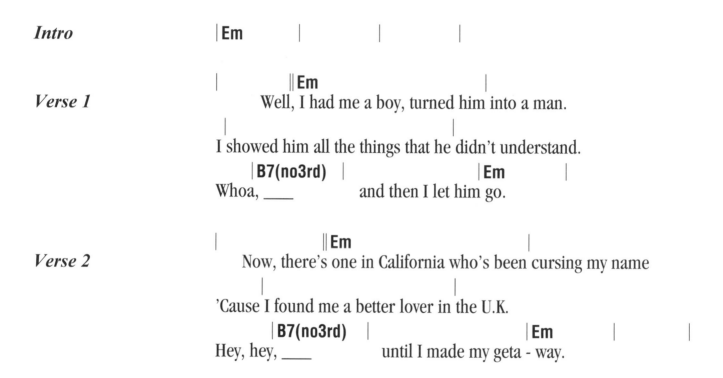

**Intro** |Em | | |

**Verse 1**
| ‖Em |
Well, I had me a boy, turned him into a man.
| |
I showed him all the things that he didn't understand.
|B7(no3rd) | |Em |
Whoa, ___ and then I let him go.

**Verse 2**
| ‖Em |
Now, there's one in California who's been cursing my name
| |
'Cause I found me a better lover in the U.K.
|B7(no3rd) | |Em | |
Hey, hey, ___ until I made my geta - way.

*Pre-Chorus 1*

‖ **Em**  **N.C.**             |

One, ___ two, three, they gonna run back to me

    |                    |              |

'Cause I'm the best baby that they never gotta keep.

    |                    |

One, two, three, they gonna run back to me.

    | **Em**  **N.C.**             |              |

They al - ways wanna come, but they never wanna leave.

*Chorus 1*

‖ **G**        | **D**           | **Em**

Exes and the oh, oh, oh's they haunt ___ me.

    | **B**              | **G**           | **D**

Like ghosts they want ___ me to make 'em oh, oh, oh.

    | **A**     | **C**       | **Em**    |        |        |        |

They won't let go. Exes and oh's.

*Verse 3*

‖ **Em**                |

Had a summer lover down in New Orleans.

    |                          |

Kept him warm in the winter, left him frozen in the spring.

    | **B7(no3rd)**    |                      | **Em**        |              |

My, my, ___            how the seasons go by.

*Verse 4*

‖ **Em**          |

I get high, and I love to get low,

    |                          |

So the hearts keep breaking and the heads just roll.

    | **B7(no3rd)**    |                      | **Em**        |              |

You know, ___            that's how the story goes.

*Pre-Chorus 2*          *Repeat Pre-Chorus 1*

*Chorus 2*

‖**G**      |**D**            |**Em**
Exes and the oh, oh, oh's they haunt ___ me.
  |**B**          |**G**         |**D**
Like ghosts they want ___ me to make 'em oh, oh, oh.
    |**A**   |**C**
They won't let go.
      |**G**      |**D**            |**Em**
My ex - es and the oh, oh, oh's they haunt ___ me.
    |**B**        |**G**       |**D**
Like ghosts they want ___ me to make 'em oh, oh, oh.
     |**A**   |**C**
They won't let go. Exes and…

*Guitar Solo*

‖**Em**        |        |        |
 Oh's.
|**B7(no3rd)**  |       |**Em**     |     |

*Pre-Chorus 1*

‖**Em N.C.**         |      |
     One, two, three, they gonna run back to me
|                |           |
Climbing over mountains and, uh, sailing over seas.
|          |
One, two, three, they gonna run back to me.
   |**Em N.C.**       |
They al - ways wanna come, but they never wanna leave.

*Chorus 3*

    ‖**G**      |**D**          |**Em**
My ex - es and the oh, oh, oh's they haunt ___ me.
    |**B**        |**G**       |**D**
Like ghosts they want ___ me to make 'em oh, oh, oh.
   |**A**   |**C**
They won't let go.
 |**G**      |**D**          |**Em**
Ex - es and the oh, oh, oh's they haunt ___ me.
   |**B**       |**G**     |**D**
Like ghosts they want ___ me to make 'em oh, oh, oh.
    |**A**   |**C**   |**Em**   |   |   |**N.C.**  ‖
They won't let go. Exes and oh's.

# Hello

Words and Music by
Adele Adkins and Greg Kurstin

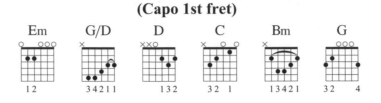

**(Capo 1st fret)**

Em     G/D     D     C     Bm     G

*Intro*

| Em     G/D     | D     C

*Verse 1*

‖Em  G/D     |D   C
Hel - lo,       it's me.
|Em       G/D                    |D
I was won - dering if after all these years
          C              |Em  G/D          |D   C
You'd like to meet to go o - ver    everything.
                        |Em            G/D
They say that time's ___ supposed to heal ya,
          |D          C
But I ain't done much healing.

*Verse 2*

‖Em  G/D              |D          C
Hel - lo,       can you hear ___ me?
|Em       G/D                         |D          C
I'm in Cal - ifor - nia, dreaming about who ___ we used to be
                    |Em  G/D   |D   C
When we were young - er     and free.
          |Em       G/D                      |D            C
I've forgot - ten how it felt before the world ___ fell at our ___ feet.
                |Em       D   |Bm   C
There's such a diff'rence    be - tween us
     |Em   D   C   |          |
And a milli - on miles.

*Chorus 1*

```
  || Em         C           | G      D
       Hello from the other side.
   | Em              C              | G      D
   I must have called a thousand times
           | Em      C           | G            D
   To tell you ____ I'm sorry for ev'ry - thing that I've done
                     | Em     C  | G        D    |
   But when I call ____ you never seem to be home.
   | Em        C         | G     D
      Hello from the outside.
     | Em          C           | G      D
   At least I can say that I've tried
           | Em     C     | G            D
   To tell you ____ I'm sorry for breaking your heart.
                   | Em   C            |
   But it don't mat - ter it clearly doesn't
   | G           D            | Em   G/D  | D    C
      Tear you a - part anymore.
```

*Verse 3*

```
        || Em   G/D        | D        C
   Hel - lo,      how are ____ you?
        | Em     G/D            | D        C
   It's so typical of me to talk about ____ myself, I'm sorry.
        | Em   G/D         | D    C
   I hope ____    that you're well.
           | Em         G/D
   Did you ev - er make it ____ out of that town
           | D         C
   Where noth - ing ever ____ happened?
        | Em    D     | Bm    C
   It's no secret    that the both of us
     | Em      D    C    |
   Are running out of time.
```

*Chorus 2*

```
 ‖Em         C            |G   D
So, hello from the other side.
 |Em              C            |G    D
I must have called a thousand times
           |Em       C           |G              D
To tell you ____ I'm sorry for ev'ry - thing that I've done
                       |Em    C  |G           D     |
But when I call ____ you never seem to be home.
|Em          C         |G   D
 Hello from the outside.
  |Em          C               |G    D
At least I can say that I've tried
           |Em       C      |G             D
To tell you ____ I'm sorry for breaking your heart.
                     |Em  C                 |
But it don't mat - ter it clearly doesn't
|G              D           |Em   C
 Tear you a - part anymore.
        |D    G          |Em   C
Ooh, _____ anymore.
        |D    G          |Em   C
Ooh, _____ anymore.
        |D    G          |Em   C           |D      |
Ooh, _____ anymore. ____     Anymore.
```

*Chorus 3*

```
 ‖Em          C           |G   D
 Hello from the other side.
 |Em                C               |G    D
I must have called a thousand times
           |Em       C              |G              D
To tell you ____ I'm sorry for ev'ry - thing that I've done
                       |Em     C   |G           D     |
But when I call ____ you never seem to be home.
|Em          C         |G   D
 Hello from the outside.
 |Em          C                 |G    D
At least I can say that I've tried
           |Em       C      |G              D
To tell you ____ I'm sorry for breaking your heart.
                     |Em   C                 |
But it don't mat - ter it clearly doesn't
|G              D           |Em   G/D  |D   C  |Em      ‖
 Tear you a - part anymore.
```

# Let It Go

Words and Music by
James Bay and Paul Barry

Tune down 1 step:
(low to high) D-G-C-F-A-D

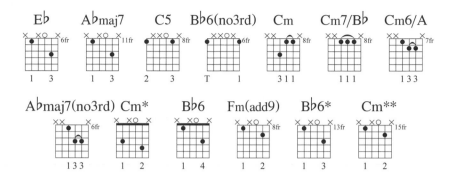

**Intro**
‖: E♭ A♭maj7 | C5 B♭6(no3rd) :‖

**Verse 1**
‖E♭ A♭maj7 | C5 B♭6(no3rd) |
From walking home ____ and talking loads,
|E♭ A♭maj7 |C5 B♭6(no3rd) |
Seeing shows ____ in evening clothes with you.
|E♭ A♭maj7 |C5 B♭6(no3rd) |
From nervous touch ____ and getting drunk
|E♭ A♭maj7 |C5 B♭6(no3rd) |
To staying up ____ and waking up with you.

**Pre-Chorus 1**
‖Cm Cm7/B♭
But now we're sleeping at the edge,
|Cm6/A A♭maj7(no3rd)
Holding something we don't need.
|Cm Cm7/B♭
All this de - lusion in our heads
|Cm6/A
Is gonna bring us to our knees.

**Chorus 1**

‖ A♭maj7   E♭
So come on, let it go.

| Cm*   B♭6
Just let it be.

| Fm(add9)   E♭                              | B♭6
Why don't you be you _____ and I'll be me?

| A♭maj7   E♭                          | Cm*   B♭6
Ev'rything that's broke, _____ leave it to the breeze.

| Fm(add9)   E♭                      | B♭6                              |
Why don't you be you _____ and I'll be me, ___ and I'll be me?


**Interlude 1**          *Repeat Intro*


**Verse 2**

‖ E♭                              A♭maj7                    | C5   B♭6(no3rd)   |
     From throwing clothes ____ across the floor

| E♭                              A♭maj7                          | C5   B♭6(no3rd)   |
     To teeth and claws ____ and slamming doors at you.

| E♭          A♭maj7                    | C5   B♭6(no3rd)
     If this is all ____ we're living for

          | E♭                          A♭maj7                | C5   B♭6(no3rd)
Why are we doing it, doing it, doing it anymore?


**Pre-Chorus 2**

          ‖ Cm                    Cm7/B♭
I used to recognize myself,

                              | Cm6/A        A♭maj7(no3rd)
It's funny how reflections change.

                    | Cm                              Cm7/B♭
When we're be - coming something else

                              | Cm6/A
I think it's time to walk away.


**Chorus 2**          *Repeat Chorus 1*

*Interlude 2*        *Repeat Intro*


*Bridge*
     ‖**Fm(add9)**                |**E♭**
        Try to fit your hand inside of mine
                              |
When we know it just don't belong.
|**B♭6***                                  |**Cm***            |
        There's no force on earth could make it feel right, ____ no. Whoa.
|**Fm(add9)**                |**E♭**
        Try to push this problem up the hill
                            |
When it's just too heavy to hold.
|**B♭6***                     |**Cm****
        Think now's the time to let it slide.


*Chorus 3*
                         ‖**A♭maj7**   **E♭**
So come on, let it go, oh.
               |**Cm***   **B♭6**
Just let it be.
                    |**Fm(add9)**   **E♭**         |**B♭6**
Why don't you be you _____ and I'll be me?
                 |**A♭maj7**   **E♭**         |**Cm***   **B♭6**
Ev'rything that's broke, _____ leave it to the breeze.
                |**Fm(add9)**   **E♭**       |**B♭6**
Let the ashes fall, _____ forget about me.
                 |**A♭maj7**   **E♭**      |**Cm***   **B♭6**
Come on, let it go. _____ Just let it be.
                |**Fm(add9)**   **E♭**         |**B♭6**       |
Why don't you be you _____ and I'll be me, ____ and I'll be me?


*Outro*
     ‖:**E♭**   **A♭maj7**   |**C5**   **B♭6(no3rd)** :‖ **E♭**        ‖

# Like I'm Gonna Lose You

Words and Music by
Caitlyn Elizabeth Smith, Justin Weaver
and Meghan Trainor

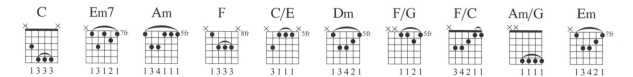

**Verse 1**

||C          |Em7      |
*Female:*  I found myself dreaming  in silver and gold,

|Am            |F C/E Dm F/G |
Like a scene from a movie that ev'ry broken heart knows.

|C     F/C C  |Em7        |
We were walking on moonlight,  and you pulled me close.

|Am        Am/G    |F C/E Dm F/G |
Split second and you disap - peared, and then I was all a - lone.

|C     F/C C    |
I woke up in tears  with you by my side.

|Em7         |Am    |
 Breath of relief, and I realized,

|F     C/E   Dm |
No, we're not promised to - morrow.

**Chorus 1**

  F/G  ||C      |Em   |
So, I'm gonna love you like I'm gonna lose you.

   |Am   Am/G  |F   |
I'm gonna hold you like I'm saying good - bye.

     |C        |Em  |
Wherever we're standing, I won't take you for granted,

     |Am     Am/G |F |
'Cause we'll never know when, when we'll run out of time.

    |C      |Em  |
So, I'm gonna love you like I'm gonna lose you.

  |Am   
I'm gonna love you

  Am/G   |F  C/E Dm F/G |
Like I'm gonna lose _____ you.

*Verse 2*

```
            ‖C                           |Em7                        |
```
*Male:*   In the blink of an eye,     just a whisper of smoke,

```
|Am                            |F    C/E   Dm   F/G      |
```
   You could lose ev'rything, the truth is you nev - er know.

```
|C            F/C  C         |Em7                        |
```
   So, I'll kiss you   longer, baby,     any chance that I get.

```
|Am                      Am/G        |F        C/E      Dm    F/G|
```
   I'll make the most of the minutes and love with no re - grets.

```
|C            F/C  C                |
```
 Let's take our time    to say what we want,

```
|Em7                              |Am
```
Use what we've got before it's all gone.

```
                              |F           C/E       Dm
```
'Cause no, we're not promised to - morrow.


*Chorus 2*        *Repeat Chorus 1*


*Guitar Solo*        |C          |Em7        |Am          |F    C/E   Dm


```
          F/G      ‖C                         |Em
```
*Chorus 3*        So, I'm gonna love you like I'm gonna lose you.

```
               |Am                            |F   C/E   Dm
```
I'm gonna hold you like I'm saying good - bye.

```
          F/G        |C                        |Em
```
Wher - ever we're standing, I won't take you for granted,

```
                |Am                    Am/G    |F
```
'Cause we'll never know when, when we'll run out of time.

```
                |C                    |Em
```
So, I'm gonna love you like I'm gonna lose you.

```
          |Am          Am/G    |F     C/E    Dm   F/G | C   ‖
```
I'm gonna love you like I'm gonna lose _____ you.

# Love Yourself

Words and Music by
Ed Sheeran, Benny Blanco
and Justin Bieber

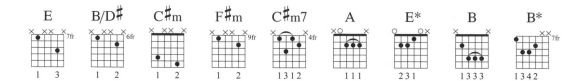

**Verse 1**

   N.C.        ‖E                B/D♯       |C♯m
For all the times ___ that you rained ___ on my pa - rade

              |F♯m          E         |B/D♯
And all the clubs ___ you get in using my name.

                     |E             B/D♯        |C♯m
You think you broke ___ my heart, oh girl for goodness ___ sake.

             |F♯m          E         |B/D♯
You think I'm cry - ing on my own, well I ain't.

**Verse 2**

                  ‖E
And I didn't want to write a song

B/D♯               |C♯m
 'Cause I didn't want anyone thinking I still care.

|F♯m      E       |B/D♯
I don't, but you still hit my phone up.

               |E      B/D♯        |C♯m
And baby, I'll be moving on    and I think it should be something

            |F♯m      E          |B/D♯
I don't wanna hold back, maybe you should know that.

**Pre-Chorus 1**

           ‖C♯m7  A         |E*

My mama don't like you, and she likes everyone.

          |C♯m7  A       |E*

And I never like to  admit that I was wrong.

          |C♯m7    A

And I've been so caught up in my job

       |E*     B     |C♯m7  A

Didn't see what's go - ing on and now I know,

        |B*

I'm better sleeping on my own.

**Chorus 1**

     N.C.    ‖E*     B   |C♯m7

'Cause if you like the way ____ you look that much,

A   |E*          A   |E*

Oh, baby, you should go and love yourself.

         |       B  |C♯m7   A

And if you think that I'm ____ still holding on to something,

|E*         A  |E*

 You should go and love yourself.

**Verse 3**

          ‖E     B/D♯  |C♯m

But when you told ____ me that you hated my friends,

         |F♯m     E      |B/D♯

The only prob - lem was with you and not them.

         |E     B/D♯     |C♯m

And ev'ry time ____ you told me my opinion was wrong

         |F♯m     E      |B/D♯

And tried to make ____ me forget where I came from.

**Verse 4**        *Repeat Verse 2*

**Pre-Chorus 2**     *Repeat Pre-Chorus 1*

**Chorus 2**       *Repeat Chorus 1*

**Horn Solo**

```
‖E*    B    |C#m7 A  |E*    A   |E*           |
|      B    |C#m7 A  |E*    A   |E*   N.C.
```

**Verse 5**

```
                        ‖E              B/D#        |C#m
For all the times ___ that you made ___ me feel small,
            |F#m          E          |B/D#
I fell in love, ___ now I feel nothing at all.
            |E              B/D#        |C#m
I never felt ___ so low when I was vulnera - ble.
            |F#m          E                  |B/D#
Was I a fool ___ to let you break down my walls?
```

**Chorus 3**

*Repeat Chorus 1*

**Outro-Chorus**

```
            ‖E*            B   |C#m7
'Cause if you like the way ___ you look that much,
A      |E*                      A      |E*
Oh, baby, you should go and love  yourself.
            |              B   |C#m        A              |
And if you think that I'm ___ still holding on to something,
|E*                       A    |E*        ‖
 You should go and love yourself.
```

# Perfect

Words and Music by
Harry Styles, Louis Tomlinson,
John Henry Ryan, Jesse Shatkin,
Maureen McDonald, Jacob Hindlin
and Julian Bunetta

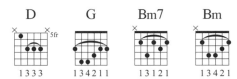

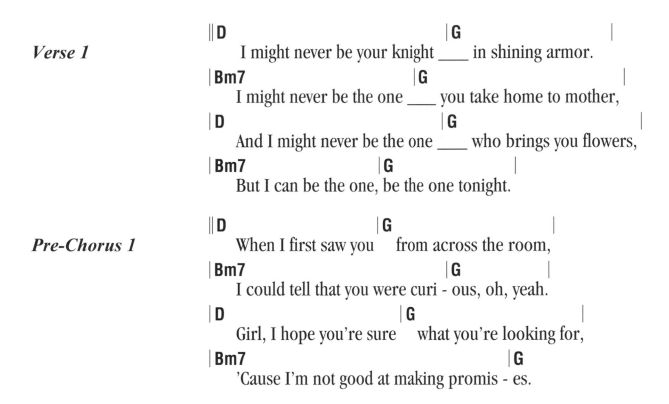

*Verse 1*

‖D                                    |G                    |
    I might never be your knight ___ in shining armor.

|Bm7                          |G                          |
    I might never be the one ___ you take home to mother,

|D                                      |G                    |
    And I might never be the one ___ who brings you flowers,

|Bm7                    |G                  |
    But I can be the one, be the one tonight.

*Pre-Chorus 1*

‖D                          |G                          |
    When I first saw you     from across the room,

|Bm7                              |G                |
    I could tell that you were curi - ous, oh, yeah.

|D                            |G                  |
    Girl, I hope you're sure     what you're looking for,

|Bm7                                        |G          |
    'Cause I'm not good at making promis - es.

**Chorus 1**

```
       ‖ D                              |
But if you like causing trouble up in hotel rooms
         | G                         |
And if you like having secret little rendezvous
      | Bm                              |
If you like to do the things you know that we shouldn't do,
             | G                | N.C.
Then baby, I'm perfect. Baby, I'm perfect for you.
             | D                     |
And if you like midnight driving with the windows down
        | G                        |
And if you like going places we can't even pronounce,
      | Bm                        |
If you like to do whatever you've been dreaming about,
          | G              |   N.C.          | D          |
Baby, you're perfect. Baby, you're perfect    so let's start right now.
```

**Verse 2**

```
    ‖ D                         | G                    |
   I might never be the hands ___ you put your heart in
| Bm7                    | G                        |
   Or the arms that hold you anytime you want them.
| D                             | G                        |
   But that don't mean that we can't live ___ here in the moment,
| Bm7                    | G                    |
   'Cause I can be the one you love from time to time.
```

**Pre-Chorus 2**          *Repeat Pre-Chorus 1*

*Chorus 2*

‖**D** |
But if you like causing trouble up in hotel rooms

|**G** |
And if you like having secret little rendezvous

|**Bm** |
If you like to do the things you know that we shouldn't do,

|**G** |**N.C.**
Then baby, I'm perfect. Baby, I'm perfect for you.

|**D** |
And if you like midnight driving with the windows down

|**G** |
And if you like going places we can't even pronounce,

|**Bm** |
If you like to do whatever you've been dreaming about,

|**G** | |
Baby, you're perfect. Baby, you're perfect, so let's start right now.


*Bridge*

‖**D** | |**G** |
And if you like camera's flashing ev'ry time we go out,    oh yeah,

| |**Bm**
   And if you're looking for someone

|
To write your breakup songs about,

|**G** |
Baby, I'm perfect. Baby we're perfect.


*Chorus 3*

‖**D** |
If you like causing trouble up in hotel rooms

|**G** |
And if you like having secret little rendezvous

|**Bm** |
If you like to do the things you know that we shouldn't do,

|**G** | **N.C.**
Then baby, I'm perfect. Baby, I'm perfect for you.

|**D** |
And if you like midnight driving with the windows down

|**G** |
And if you like going places we can't even pronounce,

|**Bm** |
If you like to do whatever you've been dreaming about,

|**G** | | ‖
Baby, you're perfect. Baby, you're perfect, so let's start right now.

# Renegades

Words and Music by
Alexander Junior Grant, Adam Levin,
Casey Harris, Noah Feldshuh
and Sam Harris

**(Capo 2nd fret)**

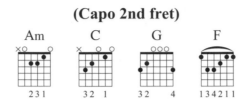

*Intro*

‖: Am | C | G | F :‖ *Play 4 times*

*Verse 1*

‖Am | C | G | F |
Run away ___ with me, (La, la, la, la, la, la, la, la, la.)
|Am | C | G | F |
Lost souls and reverie. (Hey! La, la, la, la, la, la, la, la, la.)
|Am | C | G | F |
Running wild and running free, (La, la, la, la, la, la, la, la, la.)
|Am | C | G |
Two kids, you and me. (Hey! La, la, la, la, la, la…)

*Chorus 1*

|F ‖Am | C |
And I say, "Hey, ___ hey, hey, hey,
|G | F |
Living like ___ we're renegades.
|Am | C |
Hey, hey, hey, ___ hey, hey, hey,
|G | F |
Living like ___ we're renegades, ___ uh, renegades,
|Am | C | G | F |
Renegades."
|Am | C | G | F |

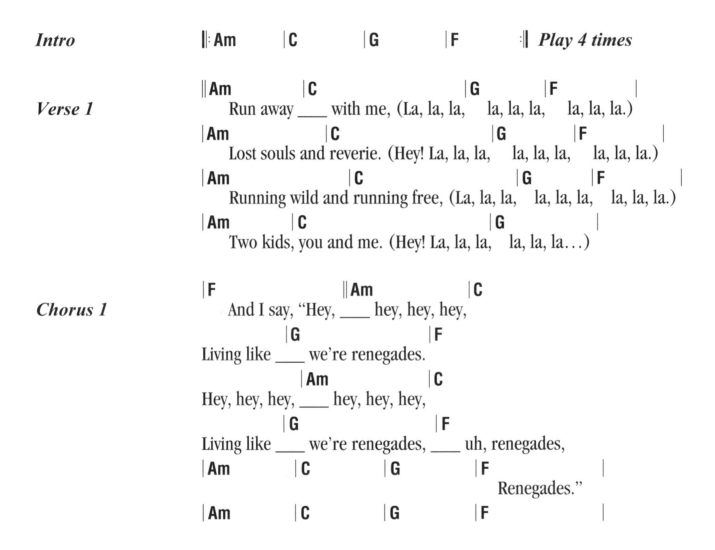

*Verse 2*

```
‖Am              |C                    |G            |F           |
    Long live the pioneers, (La, la, la,   la, la, la,   la, la, la.)
|Am              |C                    |G            |F           |
    Rebels and mutineers. (Hey! La, la, la,   la, la, la,   la, la, la.)
|Am              |C                    |G            |F           |
    Go forth and have no fear. (La, la, la,   la, la, la,   la, la, la.)
|Am              |C                    |G            |
    Come close and lend an ear. (Hey! La, la, la,   la, la, la…)
```

*Chorus 2*          *Repeat Chorus 1*

**Interlude**       ‖: Am       |C        |G        |F        :‖

*Verse 3*

```
‖Am              |C           |G            |F           |
    All hail the underdogs.    All hail the new kids.
|Am              |C       |G                |F           |
    All hail the outlaws,    Spielbergs and Kubricks.
|Am              |C           |G                |F           |
    Our time to make a move.    Our time to make amends.
|Am              |C           |G                |
    Our time to break the rules.    Let's begin.  |
```

*Chorus 3*          *Repeat Chorus 1*

**Outro**           ‖: Am       |C        |G        |F           :‖ *Play 6 times*

# She Used to Be Mine

from WAITRESS THE MUSICAL

Words and Music by
Sara Bareilles

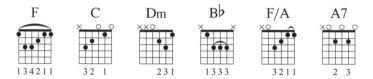

**Intro**     ‖**F**       |       |

**Verse 1**     ‖**F**       |

It's not simple to say,

  |**C**       |

Most days      I don't recognize me

  |**Dm**

With these shoes and this apron.

  |         |**B♭**

That place and its patrons have taken more

      |    **F/A** |

Than I gave ___ them.

|**F**       |

It's not easy to know,

|     |**C**       |

I'm not anything    like I used to be,

    |**Dm**

Although it's true, ___ I was never

|         |

At - tention's sweet center.

|**B♭**       |

I still remember that girl.

*Chorus 1*

        |        ‖**F**            |
She's im - perfect, but she tries.

        |**C**          |
She is good, but she lies.

       |**Dm**        |
She is hard on herself.

|      |**B♭**                  |
She is broken and won't ask for help.

|       |**F**            |
She is messy, but she's kind.

       |**C**         |
She is lonely      most of the time.

      |**Dm**             |           |**B♭**
She is all of this, mixed up and baked in a beautiful pie.

        |           |**F**      |       |
She is gone but she used to be mine.

*Verse 2*

        ‖**F**               |
    It's not what I asked ____ for.

|        |**C**         |
Sometimes life      just slips in through a back door

    |**Dm**            |          |**B♭**
And carves out a person and makes you believe it's all true.

        |           |
And now I've got you.

|**F**               |
    And you're not what I asked ____ for.

      |**A7**          |
If I'm hon - est, I know I would give it all back

       |**Dm**         |         |**B♭**
For a chance ____ to start over and rewrite an ending or two

      |
For the girl that I knew,

*Chorus 2*

‖ **F** |
Who'd be reckless, just e - nough,

|**C** |
Who'd get hurt, ___  but who learns how to toughen up

|**Dm** |  |**B♭**
When she's bruised  and gets used by a man who can't love.

| |**F**
And then she'll get stuck, and be scared

| |**A7**
Of the life that's inside her, growing stronger each day,

| |**Dm**
'Til it fin'lly reminds her to fight just a little

| |**B♭**
To bring back the fire in her eyes

| |**F** | |
That's been gone, but used to be mine,

|**A7** | |**Dm** |
Used to be mine.

| |**B♭** |

*Outro*

| ‖ **F** |
She is messy, but she's kind.

|**C** |
She is lonely  most of the time.

|**Dm** | |**B♭**
She is all of this, mixed up and baked in a beautiful pie.

| |**F** ‖
She is gone, but she used to be mine.

# Stitches

Words and Music by
Teddy Geiger, Danny Parker
and Daniel Kyriakides

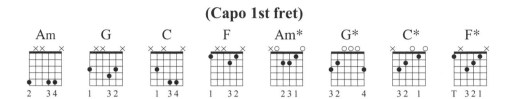

(Capo 1st fret)

Am    G    C    F    Am*    G*    C*    F*

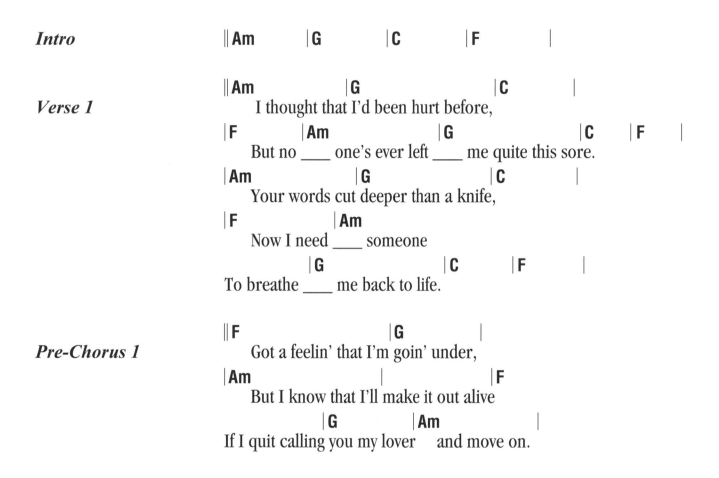

**Intro** ‖Am |G |C |F |

**Verse 1**
‖Am |G |C |
    I thought that I'd been hurt before,
|F |Am |G |C |F |
    But no ___ one's ever left ___ me quite this sore.
|Am |G |C |
    Your words cut deeper than a knife,
|F |Am |
    Now I need ___ someone
                |G |C |F |
To breathe ___ me back to life.

**Pre-Chorus 1**
‖F |G |
    Got a feelin' that I'm goin' under,
|Am | |F |
    But I know that I'll make it out alive
              |G |Am |
If I quit calling you my lover    and move on.

**Chorus 1**

|G              ‖ Am*                     |
You watch me bleed until I can't breathe,
|G*           |C*            |
Shaking, falling onto my knees.
|F*         |Am*               |G*    |
And now that I'm without your kiss  -  es,
|F*               |C*  G* |
 I'll be needing stitch   -   es.
|Am*              |G*        |C*              |
Tripping over myself,     aching, begging you to come help.
|F*           |Am*             |G*     |
And now that I'm without your kiss  -  es
|F*               |C*  G* |
 I'll be needing stitch   -   es.

**Verse 2**

‖Am*      |G*                   |C*       |
Just like a moth drawn to a flame,
|F*           |Am*         |
Oh, you lured ____ me in,
    |G*              |C*        |F*     |
I could - n't sense the pain.
|Am*              |G*             |C*        |
Your bitter heart, ____ cold to the touch.
|F*               |Am*           |
Now, I'm gonna reap ____ what I sow.
|G*              |C*         |F*     |
I'm left seein' red ____ on my own.

**Pre-Chorus 2**

‖F                 |G*         |
Got a feelin' that I'm goin' under,
|Am*             |                 |F*    |
But I know that I'll make it out alive
          |G*        |Am*         |
If I quit calling you my lover    and move on.

**Chorus 2**              *Repeat Chorus 1*

*Interlude*  ‖ **Am\*  G\***│        **C\***│        **F\***│            │

*Bridge*  ‖: **Am\***                    **G\***│                    **C\***│
Needle and thread, got - ta   get you out of my head,
│                                **F\***│                    :‖ *Play 3 times*
Needle and the thread, gon - na   wind up dead.
│**Am\***                    **G\***│                    **C\***│
Needle and thread, got - ta get you out of my head,
│                    **N.C.**   │
Get you out of my head.

*Chorus 3*  │                    ‖**Am\***                    │
You watch me bleed until I can't breathe,
│**G\***        │**C\***                    │
Shaking, falling onto my knees.
│**F\***            │**Am\***                    │**G\***        │
And now that I'm without your kiss  -  es,
│**F\***                    │**C\* G\***│
I'll be needing stitch   -   es.
│**Am\***                    │**G\***        │**C\***                    │
Tripping over myself,     aching, begging you to come help.
│**F\***            │**Am\***                    │**G\***        │
And now that I'm without your kiss  -  es
│**F\***                    │**C\* G\***
I'll be needing stitch   -   es.
│**N.C.**                    │        │
Now that I'm without your kiss - es,
│                    │
I'll be needing stitch - es.
│                    │        │
Now that I'm without your kiss - es,
│                    │        ‖
I'll be needing stitch - es.

# (Smooth As) Tennessee Whiskey

Words and Music by
Dean Dillon and Linda Hargrove

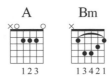

**Intro**   ‖A      |Bm      |      |A      |

**Verse 1**   ‖A                          |Bm      |
Used to spend my nights out in bar - rooms.
|                          |A      |
Liquor was the only love I'd known.
|                          |Bm
But you rescued me from reachin' for the bottom
        |                          |A
And brought me back from bein' too far gone.

**Chorus 1**   ‖A                          |Bm
You're as smooth as Tennessee whiskey,
        |                          |A
You're as sweet as strawberry wine.
        |                          |Bm
You're as warm ____ as a glass of brandy,
        |                          |A      |
And, honey, I stay stoned on your love all the time.

**Verse 2**   ‖A                          |Bm      |
I've looked for love in all the same old plac - es.
|                          |A      |
Found the bottom of a bottle's always dry.
|                          |Bm
But when you poured out your heart, I didn't waste it,
        |                          |A
'Cause there's nothin' ____ like your love to get me high.

*Chorus 2*

‖**A**                                              |**Bm**
And, you're as smooth as Tennessee whiskey,

|                                    |**A**
You're as sweet as strawberry wine.

|                          |**Bm**
You're as warm ___ as a glass of brandy,

|                                        |**A**          |
And, honey, I stay stoned on your love all the time.


**Guitar Solo**          *Repeat Verse 1 (Instrumental)*


‖**A**                              |**Bm**
*Chorus 3*      You're as smooth as Tennessee whiskey,

|                          |**A**
You're as sweet as strawberry wine.

|                          |**Bm**
You're as warm ___ as a glass of brandy,

|                                  |**A**
And, honey, I stay stoned on your love all the time.

|                          |**Bm**
You're as smooth as Tennessee whiskey,

|                          |**A**
Tennessee whiskey, ___ Tennessee whiskey.

|                          |**Bm**
You're as smooth as Tennessee whiskey,

|                          |**A**          ‖
Tennessee whiskey, ___ Tennessee whiskey.

# Tear in My Heart

Words and Music by
Tyler Joseph

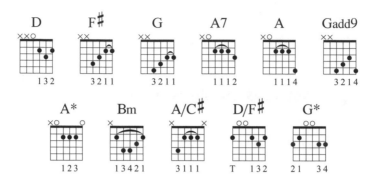

**Intro**

‖N.C. |D F♯ G |N.C. |

*Ahn nyang ha se yo.*

**Verse 1**

‖D F♯ G |N.C. |D F♯ G |

Sometimes you gotta bleed to know

|N.C. |D F♯ G |

That you're alive and have a soul.

|N.C. |A7 |

But it takes someone to come a - round to show you how.

**Chorus 1**

|A ‖Gadd9 |

She's the tear in my heart, I'm alive.

| A* |Bm |

She's the tear in my heart, I'm on fi - re.

A/C♯ |D |A* N.C. |

She's the tear in my heart, take me high - er than I've ever been.

**Verse 2**

```
||D   F♯   G  |                                    |D        F♯    G  |
                    The songs on the radio are okay,
|N.C.                      |D      F♯   G  |
     But my taste in music is your face.
|N.C.                          |A7                  |
     And it takes a song to come a - round to show you how.
```

**Chorus 2**

```
|A                       ||Gadd9           |
     She's the tear in my heart, I'm alive.
|            A*      |Bm            |
     She's the tear in my heart, I'm on fi - re.
        A/C♯    |D             |A*                 |
She's the tear in my heart, take me high - er than I've ever been.
|Gadd9         |          A*         |
             Than I've ever been,
|Bm           |          A/C♯           |D        |
             Than I've ___ ever been,
|A*                        |
     Than I've ever been.
```

**Bridge**

```
||D          |          |        D/F♯  G*  |D    |
(Oh, oh, oh, oh.        Oo, oo, ____  oo,  oo.)
|              D/F♯    G*   |D                     |
     You fell a - sleep in my      car, I drove the whole time.
|              D/F♯    G*   |D                      |
     But that's o - kay, I'll just a - void the holes so you sleep fine.
|              D/F♯    G*   |D                  |
     I'm driving, here I sit      cursing my government
|              D/F♯    G*   |D                      |
     For not us - ing my taxes to fill holes with more cement.
|              D/F♯    G*   |D                     |
     You fell a - sleep in my      car, I drove the whole time.
|              D/F♯    G*   |D                       |
     But that's o - kay, I'll just a - void the holes so you sleep fine.
|              D/F♯   G*  |D                  |
     I'm driving, here I sit      cursing my government
|A7                     |A                    |
     For not using my taxes to fill holes with more cement.
```

**Verse 3**        *Repeat Verse 1*

*Chorus 3*

```
|A                    ‖Gadd9            |
   She's the tear in my heart, I'm alive.
|            A*      |Bm              |
   She's the tear in my heart, I'm on fi - re.
          A/C♯     |D              |A*        N.C.
She's the tear in my heart, take me high - er than I've ever been.
 |Gadd9          |              A*      |Bm              |
My heart is my ar - mor. She's the tear in my heart, she's a car - ver.
         A/C♯          |D            |A*              |
She's a butcher with a smile, cut me far - ther than I've ever been,
|Gadd9        |            A*      |Bm              |
             Than I've ever been.
|            A/C♯        |D        |A*
   Than I've ever been,        oh, ___ than I've ever been.
```

*Outro-Chorus*

```
            ‖G*          |              A*      |Bm              |
My heart is my ar - mor. She's the tear in my heart, she's a car - ver.
         A/C♯          |D            |A*            |         D ‖
She's a butcher with a smile, cut me far - ther than I've ever been.
```

# Guitar Chord Songbooks

## Each 6" x 9" book includes complete lyrics, chord symbols, and guitar chord diagrams.

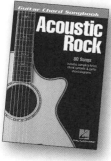 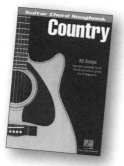 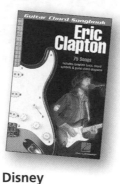 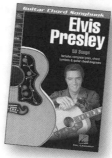

**Acoustic Hits**
00701787 . . . . . . . . . . . . . . . . . . . . . . . $14.99
**Acoustic Rock**
00699540 . . . . . . . . . . . . . . . . . . . . . . . $17.95
**Adele**
00102761 . . . . . . . . . . . . . . . . . . . . . . . $14.99
**Alabama**
00699914 . . . . . . . . . . . . . . . . . . . . . . . $14.95
**The Beach Boys**
00699566 . . . . . . . . . . . . . . . . . . . . . . . $14.95
**The Beatles (A-I)**
00699558 . . . . . . . . . . . . . . . . . . . . . . . $17.99
**The Beatles (J-Y)**
00699562 . . . . . . . . . . . . . . . . . . . . . . . $17.99
**Bluegrass**
00702585 . . . . . . . . . . . . . . . . . . . . . . . $14.99
**Blues**
00699733 . . . . . . . . . . . . . . . . . . . . . . . $12.95
**Broadway**
00699920 . . . . . . . . . . . . . . . . . . . . . . . $14.99
**Johnny Cash**
00699648 . . . . . . . . . . . . . . . . . . . . . . . $17.99
**Steven Curtis Chapman**
00700702 . . . . . . . . . . . . . . . . . . . . . . . $17.99
**Children's Songs**
00699539 . . . . . . . . . . . . . . . . . . . . . . . $16.99
**Christmas Carols**
00699536 . . . . . . . . . . . . . . . . . . . . . . . $12.99
**Christmas Songs – 2nd Edition**
00119911 . . . . . . . . . . . . . . . . . . . . . . . $14.99
**Eric Clapton**
00699567 . . . . . . . . . . . . . . . . . . . . . . . $15.99
**Classic Rock**
00699598 . . . . . . . . . . . . . . . . . . . . . . . $15.99
**Coffeehouse Hits**
00703318 . . . . . . . . . . . . . . . . . . . . . . . $14.99
**Country**
00699534 . . . . . . . . . . . . . . . . . . . . . . . $14.99
**Country Favorites**
00700609 . . . . . . . . . . . . . . . . . . . . . . . $14.99
**Country Hits**
00140859 . . . . . . . . . . . . . . . . . . . . . . . $14.99
**Country Standards**
00700608 . . . . . . . . . . . . . . . . . . . . . . . $12.95
**Cowboy Songs**
00699636 . . . . . . . . . . . . . . . . . . . . . . . $12.95
**Creedence Clearwater Revival**
00701786 . . . . . . . . . . . . . . . . . . . . . . . $12.99
**Crosby, Stills & Nash**
00701609 . . . . . . . . . . . . . . . . . . . . . . . $12.99
**John Denver**
02501697 . . . . . . . . . . . . . . . . . . . . . . . $14.99
**Neil Diamond**
00700606 . . . . . . . . . . . . . . . . . . . . . . . $14.99

**Disney**
00701071 . . . . . . . . . . . . . . . . . . . . . . . $14.99
**The Best of Bob Dylan**
14037617 . . . . . . . . . . . . . . . . . . . . . . . $17.99
**Eagles**
00122917 . . . . . . . . . . . . . . . . . . . . . . . $16.99
**Early Rock**
00699916 . . . . . . . . . . . . . . . . . . . . . . . $14.99
**Folksongs**
00699541 . . . . . . . . . . . . . . . . . . . . . . . $12.95
**Folk Pop Rock**
00699651 . . . . . . . . . . . . . . . . . . . . . . . $14.95
**40 Easy Strumming Songs**
00115972 . . . . . . . . . . . . . . . . . . . . . . . $14.99
**Four Chord Songs**
00701611 . . . . . . . . . . . . . . . . . . . . . . . $12.99
**Glee**
00702501 . . . . . . . . . . . . . . . . . . . . . . . $14.99
**Gospel Hymns**
00700463 . . . . . . . . . . . . . . . . . . . . . . . $14.99
**Grand Ole Opry®**
00699885 . . . . . . . . . . . . . . . . . . . . . . . $16.95
**Green Day**
00103074 . . . . . . . . . . . . . . . . . . . . . . . $12.99
**Guitar Chord Songbook White Pages**
00702609 . . . . . . . . . . . . . . . . . . . . . . . $29.99
**Irish Songs**
00701044 . . . . . . . . . . . . . . . . . . . . . . . $14.99
**Billy Joel**
00699632 . . . . . . . . . . . . . . . . . . . . . . . $15.99
**Elton John**
00699732 . . . . . . . . . . . . . . . . . . . . . . . $15.99
**Ray LaMontagne**
00130337 . . . . . . . . . . . . . . . . . . . . . . . $12.99
**Latin Songs**
00700973 . . . . . . . . . . . . . . . . . . . . . . . $14.99
**Love Songs**
00701043 . . . . . . . . . . . . . . . . . . . . . . . $14.99
**Bob Marley**
00701704 . . . . . . . . . . . . . . . . . . . . . . . $12.99
**Bruno Mars**
00125332 . . . . . . . . . . . . . . . . . . . . . . . $12.99
**Paul McCartney**
00385035 . . . . . . . . . . . . . . . . . . . . . . . $16.95
**Steve Miller**
00701146 . . . . . . . . . . . . . . . . . . . . . . . $12.99

**Modern Worship**
00701801 . . . . . . . . . . . . . . . . . . . . . . . $16.99
**Motown**
00699734 . . . . . . . . . . . . . . . . . . . . . . . $16.95
**The 1950s**
00699922 . . . . . . . . . . . . . . . . . . . . . . . $14.99
**The 1980s**
00700551 . . . . . . . . . . . . . . . . . . . . . . . $16.99
**Nirvana**
00699762 . . . . . . . . . . . . . . . . . . . . . . . $16.99
**Roy Orbison**
00699752 . . . . . . . . . . . . . . . . . . . . . . . $12.95
**Peter, Paul & Mary**
00103013 . . . . . . . . . . . . . . . . . . . . . . . $12.99
**Tom Petty**
00699883 . . . . . . . . . . . . . . . . . . . . . . . $15.99
**Pop/Rock**
00699538 . . . . . . . . . . . . . . . . . . . . . . . $14.95
**Praise & Worship**
00699634 . . . . . . . . . . . . . . . . . . . . . . . $14.99
**Elvis Presley**
00699633 . . . . . . . . . . . . . . . . . . . . . . . $14.95
**Queen**
00702395 . . . . . . . . . . . . . . . . . . . . . . . $12.99
**Rascal Flatts**
00130951 . . . . . . . . . . . . . . . . . . . . . . . $12.99
**Red Hot Chili Peppers**
00699710 . . . . . . . . . . . . . . . . . . . . . . . $16.95
**Rock Ballads**
00701034 . . . . . . . . . . . . . . . . . . . . . . . $14.99
**Rock 'n' Roll**
00699535 . . . . . . . . . . . . . . . . . . . . . . . $14.95
**Bob Seger**
00701147 . . . . . . . . . . . . . . . . . . . . . . . $12.99
**Carly Simon**
00121011 . . . . . . . . . . . . . . . . . . . . . . . $14.99
**Singer/Songwriter Songs**
00126053 . . . . . . . . . . . . . . . . . . . . . . . $14.99
**Sting**
00699921 . . . . . . . . . . . . . . . . . . . . . . . $14.99
**Taylor Swift**
00701799 . . . . . . . . . . . . . . . . . . . . . . . $15.99
**Three Chord Acoustic Songs**
00123860 . . . . . . . . . . . . . . . . . . . . . . . $14.99
**Three Chord Songs**
00699720 . . . . . . . . . . . . . . . . . . . . . . . $12.95
**Today's Hits**
00120983 . . . . . . . . . . . . . . . . . . . . . . . $14.99
**Top 100 Hymns Guitar Songbook**
75718017 . . . . . . . . . . . . . . . . . . . . . . . $14.99
**Two-Chord Songs**
00119236 . . . . . . . . . . . . . . . . . . . . . . . $14.99
**Ultimate-Guitar**
00702617 . . . . . . . . . . . . . . . . . . . . . . . $24.99
**U2**
00137744 . . . . . . . . . . . . . . . . . . . . . . . $14.99
**Wedding Songs**
00701005 . . . . . . . . . . . . . . . . . . . . . . . $14.99
**Hank Williams**
00700607 . . . . . . . . . . . . . . . . . . . . . . . $14.99
**Stevie Wonder**
00120862 . . . . . . . . . . . . . . . . . . . . . . . $14.99
**Neil Young–Decade**
00700464 . . . . . . . . . . . . . . . . . . . . . . . $14.99

Prices, contents, and availability subject to change without notice.

**HAL•LEONARD®**
**CORPORATION**
7777 W. BLUEMOUND RD. P.O. BOX 13819 MILWAUKEE, WI 53213

Visit Hal Leonard online at **www.halleonard.com**

0915

## STRUM & SING

*Lyrics, chord symbols, and guitar chord diagrams for your favorite songs.*

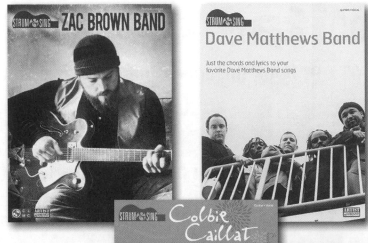

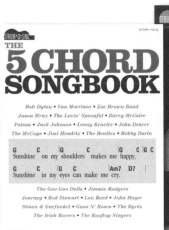

# GUITAR

**SARA BAREILLES**
00102354.................................$12.99

**ZAC BROWN BAND**
02501620.................................$12.99

**COLBIE CAILLAT**
02501725.................................$14.99

**CAMPFIRE FOLK SONGS**
02500686.................................$10.99

**CHART HITS OF 2014-2015**
00142554.................................$12.99

**BEST OF KENNY CHESNEY**
00142457.................................$14.99

**JOHN DENVER COLLECTION**
02500632.................................$9.95

**EASY ACOUSTIC SONGS**
00125478.................................$12.99

**50 CHILDREN'S SONGS**
02500825.................................$7.95

**THE 5 CHORD SONGBOOK**
02501718.................................$10.99

**FOLK SONGS**
02501482.................................$9.99

**FOLK/ROCK FAVORITES**
02501669.................................$9.99

**40 POP/ROCK HITS**
02500633.................................$9.95

**THE 4 CHORD SONGBOOK**
02501533.................................$10.99

**THE 4-CHORD COUNTRY SONGBOOK**
00114936.................................$12.99

**HITS OF THE '60S**
02501138.................................$10.95

**HITS OF THE '70S**
02500871.................................$9.99

**HYMNS**
02501125.................................$8.99

**JACK JOHNSON**
02500858.................................$16.99

**CAROLE KING**
00115243.................................$10.99

**DAVE MATTHEWS BAND**
02501078.................................$10.95

**JOHN MAYER**
02501636.................................$10.99

**INGRID MICHAELSON**
02501634.................................$10.99

**THE MOST REQUESTED SONGS**
02501748.................................$10.99

**JASON MRAZ**
02501452.................................$14.99

**PRAISE & WORSHIP**
00152381.................................$12.99

**ROCK AROUND THE CLOCK**
00103625.................................$12.99

**ROCK BALLADS**
02500872.................................$9.95

**ED SHEERAN**
00152016.................................$12.99

**THE 6 CHORD SONGBOOK**
02502277.................................$10.99

**CAT STEVENS**
00116827.................................$10.99

**TODAY'S HITS**
00119301.................................$10.99

**KEITH URBAN**
00118558.................................$12.99

**NEIL YOUNG – GREATEST HITS**
00138270.................................$12.99

# UKULELE

**COLBIE CAILLAT**
02501731.................................$10.99

**JOHN DENVER**
02501694.................................$10.99

**JACK JOHNSON**
02501702.................................$15.99

**JOHN MAYER**
02501706.................................$10.99

**INGRID MICHAELSON**
02501741.................................$10.99

**THE MOST REQUESTED SONGS**
02501453.................................$14.99

**JASON MRAZ**
02501753.................................$14.99

**SING-ALONG SONGS**
02501710.................................$14.99

HAL•LEONARD® CORPORATION
7777 W. BLUEMOUND RD. P.O. BOX 13819 MILWAUKEE, WI 53213

*Prices, content, and availability subject to change without notice.*